Eros' Lesson Learned

By Chelsea Jahaliel

Copyright

ISBN: 978-0-6483861-2-4

Copyright © Chelsea Bickley 2018

Chelsea Jahaliel asserts the right to be identified as the author of this work

All rights reserved. No part of this publication may be reproduced, stored in a retrieval system, or transmitted, in any form or by any means (electronic, mechanical, photocopying, recording or otherwise) without the prior written permission of the author.

The author has no control over and does not assume responsibility for any third-party websites or their contents.

Font: Charis SIL, copyright © 2018, SIL International,
https://software.sil.org/charis/
This Font Software is licensed under the SIL Open Font License, Version 1.1.

The Ebook version was published in November 2018 ISBN 978-0-6483861-3-1

Dedication

Dedicated to IAB who taught me how beautiful words can be
How passion and sensuality can be embraced in poetry
I think of you often.

Acknowledgements

Thanks to dragonhoardsbookz and norcumi who gave me the confidence to publish this book and whose helpful betas were much appreciated.

Thanks also (and always) to my husband for always being ready to provide inspiration and cheerleading and to the writers I love, for being wonderful, for being unafraid and for being yourselves.

A note from the Author

Please remember that sex is only sex when everyone involved is fully consenting. Communication is key. Keep in mind also that wonderful rule "safe, sane and consensual" (yes consent is so important I'm mentioning it twice).

If you're mine

I want to kiss you until the word leave
is the furthest thing from your mind
to touch you and love you, reduce you
to a stream of pleading incoherency
because there's nothing sweeter than
the way *pleasepleaseyesgodyes* falls
from your lips when I'm touching you
and I want to make you burn, hover
on the edge of falling apart until
your temper sparks in your eyes -
until the only thing stopping you
from rolling us over and taking is
that I asked to love you like this
Call my name, let me hear you shape the
syllables with all that love you have
I want you sated with half closed eyes and
swollen lips telling me that you're mine

Quietly between breaths

My heart in your hands
My soul in your keeping
As long as you wish it
I'm yours - *please* - *I'm yours*

Then you are

If I'm yours will you promise to be mine
let me claim you body and soul as you
did for me? Let me touch and taste my fill
until you are balancing on the edge, wanting,
as my nails trace down your body raising trails
that will sting tomorrow as sure as the bruises
you left on my thighs will ache, because this
is pleasure: in trusting, in wildness, in love
Let go - trust me, I've got you, I want this
as much as you do, to reach down and take you
in my mouth, let your hands tangle in my hair
until my name is on your lips as a prayer
that I answer with my body, with my tongue
and answer it I will until we're both gasping
for breath, until we shatter together because
there's nothing more beautiful in the world
than watching you when you come, seeing
your lips half-open and curving in a smile
your eyes with pupils blown and glittering
and I'll whisper words of love and hold you
until we fall asleep limbs all entangled

Beautiful

Hair caresses skin like silk
Eyes light up with joy and
My mouth curves in a smile
As your fingers stroke my skin
Soothing rhythm drains tension
Out of my muscles leaves me
Feeling languid, desirous of
Nothing more than the extension
Of this precious moment, being
Held in your loving arms, the
Warmth of your body surrounds me
I feel beautiful – unashamed
Of the nakedness of my body

Rain on the Roof

Rain falls, the first sign that maybe our land will survive
With it comes the cold; I huddle in my bed, but I'm not alone

You are right beside me, with my head on your chest I can hear
Your breathing, I lift my head, meet your gaze gone soft with love

The drum of heart beats picks up, I ruin the words you are forming
With a kiss pressed into your yielding lips as our hands begin to tease

Warmth overtakes us and this night I'm even more grateful for the rain
Beating loud against the tin roof – muffling, drowning out our pleasure

So others can't hear just how much I love you, to feel your body heated
and taut, to make you laugh and tease you – flirting and falling fast

But yet, nothing can compare to the pleasure of having you here
Not even the breathless plunge to pleasure can match the feeling

when we, now at leisure wrap our arms around each other
And fall asleep to the sound of the rain on the roof

Standing

It's not even a little fair
How hot you look in
All your naked glory

The spray of water
Glistening along your
Muscles - time to make
This shower steamy

The glass fogs around
Two handprints appearing
The water washes us clean

Take me and lay me down
Until my head stops spinning

Glitter in the Air

> The moment you walk through the door
> I'll push you back against it, kissing you
> The moonlight streaming in highlights
> glitter on your cheekbones - I push
> the straps of your top loose, watch as
> it catches on your breasts like art, and
> I ask if this is okay, kneel before you
> When you nod I give in and touch you
> undo tight jeans, get you naked, apart
> from your six-inch heels and the glitter on
> your skin, I will worship you with hands
> and tongue and kisses until you come
> When you push yourself up and lift your
> legs to rest yourself on my shoulders
> I swear in three languages and set myself
> back to driving you insane - the way you
> moan and sigh, the way my name drips
> off your tongue when I find that perfect angle
> turns me on so much - but this right now is
> about you, about making you feel amazing
> Because you are - I love you, I want you
> all of you; I want you to give in, stop holding
> yourself back because you're worried to hurt me
> I won't break and I will kneel here until the sun
> rises, kissing you, if that is what it takes to get
> you to let go and find your release in my arms

Call me, maybe?

                Late night Skype call by candlelight
              quiet house but for the laughter shared
                I wish you were here to touch me
               my hands are not your hands and the
            difference to me is significant enough
             but at least I can watch you watch me
              narrating all the desires I rarely voice
           in your presence (knowing you'll remember)

Worship

If it were supplication unequal that would see an end
But we are equals, partners in all things so my answer
Is yes - if this is what you wish then I will lie here on
Sheets soft as silk and let you worship me as you desire

Worship pt 2

I want this - your gifted pliancy, the way you tremble
when I press kisses to your wrists, how your breath
catches in response to my gentle worship of your beauty
I am determined to kiss every inch of your skin, to see
your hands grasp for a hold in the sheets - let's make a
slow burn fire that'll last 'til dawn. I want to find the
places on your body that make you gasp, the ones that
make you laugh - I want to see the redness my attention
raises against the paleness of your breasts, the contrast
of my hand against yours - the delicacy of your fingers
does *not* discount their strength. I'll kiss your knuckles
as the ring I gave you glitters; a promise of a lifetime of Joy
I love seeing you try to keep control, and losing the battle
because I'm persistent in seeking your pleasure above all else
Watching you bite your lip, how your eyelids flutter, the blush
on your cheeks when you let yourself watch me make love to you
it drives me half insane with need but I promised slowly
to let us both burn and I am going to take advantage of the
granted opportunity, because you are so worth this worship

Paradise

>Chase paradise with me, my love - we can keep
>Each other warm, the light in your eyes outshines
>Both sun and moon; take my hand, fingers entwining
>As our bodies move as one beneath a sky of stars

Senses

I wrap the silken scarf gently around your head
cutting off sight with the weight of a simple knot
sense the shiver that runs through you at the denial
of your sense - trust me, I whisper to your ear,
feel such joy when you smile and tell me you do
If you were responsive before now every feather
light touch, every lingering kiss causes you to sigh
to tremble - your hand reaches, finds mine
holding on, grounding yourself, when I seek out
the soft skin of your thighs to raise bruises I feel
you tighten your hand, pressed together our knuckles
are white, and I leave off my kisses to check in;
I don't want this to be too much, or not good for you
You giggle (adorable), tell me that my concern
while appreciated is unwarranted - I mustn't be
doing a good enough job if you're still multi-syllabic
Saying so gains me more laughter, the sound so sweet
your hand lets go of mine, ghosting up my arm until
you brush a thumb over my cheek in a gentle caress
using the guide of your fingers you arch up and kiss me
as if to say get back to it - so I do, with great pleasure

Honey

The liquid stickiness lies golden against your skin
when I taste it, I must ensure I leave no trace - to
that end I'll lie here licking you clean, tracing the curves
and dips of you, chasing the amber-bright honey but as
lovely as it tastes, it is nothing compared to your sweetness

Fight Me

We go down together in a tangle of limbs
the bruising strength of your fingers
allows me the confidence to tear away
at the clothes you wear, wrestling with
each other, teeth clashing; I lick the blood
from your berry-bitten lips as we vie for
dominance, over and under, your hands
rough on my breasts - my nails raking
over your arm, down towards my prize
Diverted, you flip us, the lock you use
I taught you - laughing wildly I struggle
freedom gained, quickly renew my press
for advantage enjoying the fierce lightning
flash in your eyes - the way you surge up
trying to pin me, but I'm not in the mood
to be held down and taken; *no* if you want
me, then you shall get me - all fire and fight
There's pain and pleasure and bruises sucked
into skin, as you scrape your stubble along my
cheeks, as I leave a trail of bite-bruise marks
down your chest, as you push in roughly, gasping
out *fuck* as the heat surrounds you, there's no
gentle love tonight, just the sounds of us mating,
fucking with wild abandon, with anger, and rage
And pain all yielding into the high spiral of pleasure

When you come down, I'll be here holding you still
Love like ours doesn't run from the wildness of our hearts

Blueberries

the morning after...

blueberries and waffles
a gentle hand tracing
the bruises left behind

> there's an apology on your lips
> I don't want to hear it - press
> a blueberry between them because
> having your marks on my skin
> feels divine - if it didn't, there are
> ways to ease, remove them

you swallow the apology and the berry
take another, and a bite of waffle from
my fork, and let me kiss away the juice

> *whispering I love you*

and maybe our lips are stained purple
maybe the sheets of our bed are ruined
lost in the haze of love, who cares?

> no apologies between us - tell me
> please don't stop instead, let my
> hands linger on your skin, your
> lips press love against my neck
> we have all the time in the world
> this morning, so let's stay in bed

time stretches, an endless sea
of sweet berry kisses to share
between us, and we're smiling

> *best way to start the day*

Beauty is...

that I feel beautiful when you look at me
is some sort of miracle, but the hunger in
your gaze, the reverence in your gentle hands
tracing my cellulite and scars speaks volumes
softly tell me I'm beautiful and I'll not deny it
helpless beneath the weight of your regard

set me to trembling with tender, admiring touch
kiss me until every insecurity I hold fades away
until there's nothing but the feeling of you and me
entwined, floating on this sea of bright-love-feeling
let me reach for you, show you how I feel the same
you are perfect as you are and I love you

Behind Glass

Steam

Partial reflection obscured by mist
Showing curve of hip, length of leg,
Faces turned upwards to the spray
Soapy hands gliding up and down

Laughter

Whispered secrets causing giggles
Wash my back and I'll wash yours
Eyes aglow with love and passion
Flaring here behind glass doors

Sighs

Love me and hold me as
Water beads on softest skin
Touch me and mould me
Until cold spray comes between

Our passion is not fleeting

Crimson lust made more sacred by love; paint my skin
With cool ice, followed by the warmth of your tongue
Soft cotton sheets tangle up between limbs intertwined

We exchange the vows of lovers cherishing moments
Kiss me fiercely, let's burn together hotter than stars
as we delve into realms not yet explored

Our love is the diamond-cast rainbow, full of emotions
Everything from joy to sorrow and all that comes between
My every thought is with you whether I am present or no

Morning has Broken

I wake lazily
to travelling hands
the warmth of love

Moving slowly so that each second hangs in the air
stretching and shimmering, painting the world gold
lips meet in the best kind of good morning (*silent*)

Slowly urgency builds
bodies dancing together
celebrating the new dawn

Tied

>>> soft slide of silk on skin
>>> carefully crafted knots
>>> they could slip loose but
>>> you wanted and asked

> it makes my soul sing as I
> tease and touch you, my
> own gift so precious, like
> gold but better and the
> sounds you make, make me
> wet, so maybe I'll touch
> myself instead of you

hover so close to where
you want to be, let you beg
because I love hearing you
plead, I want you under
my control - *trust me*

> I'll take care of you
> I say, lowering myself
> down watching as your
> eyes flutter closed, as bliss
> suffuses your expression

>>> watching you is joy itself
>>> ask once more, I'll give in
>>> let you come inside me
>>> kiss you lazily as you do

Rain on the Roof Pt 2.

Soft and insistent the gentle drumming
On the window panes echoes my heartbeat
Under touch of hands, skin is thrumming
To rhythm of an ancient dance complete

Love springs from wells so deep
Present in each gentle kiss of lips
We are tangled together to keep
Warmth in arms, in legs, in hips

Intensity of the storm is rising and ebbing
In uncanny echo of our passions that flare
All is impassioned haste then slow lingering
lost in awestruck wonder, in love and care

Stoke the fire, fan the flames
Secure in love, our souls complete
We crest the ever expanding waves
Rain's soft lullaby lulls us both to sleep

Begging

Beg me; I want to hear you – I want you babbling
Breathless music to my ears, seek that combination
of words that would find yourself freed from the
pain-tinged pleasure of hanging on the edge of
free-fall, and if my smile curves wickedly, well,
you asked for this and when your words falter
due to a well-timed stroke of my hand, I lean in
checking I still have your consent; you're doing
so well, so beautifully for me, love – you rest your
head on my shoulder for a moment and then
begin again, words tumbling over themselves
Some earn you a kiss, some a playful swat
finally, finally it's enough, such a little push
in the end makes you come undone I hold you
close, murmuring soft reassurances, cuddling
until you laugh and promise revenge next time

Breath

my hand on your throat
controlling your breath
subtle pressure causing
pleasure - the softness
of your skin and the
hardness of your cock
both beneath my hands
the way your eyes darken
when I press just a little
more - feel the way
you pull in air like
you're desperate for it
enjoy how you become
as desperate for me as
for the air you breathe

                I breathe in and kiss you
                make sharing our life
                a little more literal
                checking in and then
                taking a little more -
                chasing highs of pleasure
                until we both come down
                I kiss the bruises from
                your skin as you hold me

Mangoes

On a hot summer night here there's nothing quite like
stripping down, grabbing a small mountain of mangoes
then sharing them with you as we sit in the bath, sticky
sweet, the seeds discarded and when we are finished we
run cold water over us, cleaning off the juice, enjoying
how refreshed we feel, hands casually entwining

the taste of mangoes lingers in our kisses 'til morning

Speak to Me

You lean in close and tell me softly how much you love me
I cannot help how I react, my shiver as your voice roughens
when you talk about all you'd like to do to me – the way you
want to love me, touch me and I can't help but grin back, quip
something light-hearted, to try and break the tension building
your laughter rolls over me like smoke and I lose my breath
even as your fingers begin their nimble work undoing buttons
you keep speaking to me, words of adoration, of love and desire
I know I'm blushing – the heat sears through me, and I'll whisper
'don't stop' into the pauses between the river of your words
"as you wish," you murmur, in that octave that goes straight
past my brain to my every nerve ending, lighting me on fire

Lace

It's amusing to watch
your brain short-circuit
and flattering besides

this is hand-made, I say
tracing the delicate work
do you like it? Smiling

You breathe out a sigh
draw me into your arms
whispering one word

"Holy"

Prince Rupert

I love when you treat me with precious gentleness
as though I'm spun glass, but I'll tell you a secret
I won't *break*

Let's play rough

Your hands in my hair, tugging me back
Your ~~lips~~ teeth on my throat, over my pulse
makes me *want*

mark me

A kiss might be grand

Kissing you is like

- Flying
- Forgetting
- Coming home
- A Symphonic crescendo
- Everything I wanted/needed/dreamed of

I lose time and worries in the warmth of your arms
find my smile in between the lazy exchange of kisses

Thank the Stars for Internet Shopping

The old-gold leather is gorgeous against your skin
I trace the criss-cross pattern as you bat my hand away
Watching you settle our new toy, your beauty takes
my breath away - once you're happy with the fit
you lean in and kiss me gently, sliding home as
though you were made for me... a thought you
catch because you laugh, bend over and whisper
that it was made just for us, and then proceed to
make me lose my mind, time and money both well spent

Golden sunrise

Lazy mornings – greet the dawn with shared kisses
my back pressed against your front as hands wander
teasing ourselves into full awareness

When you're moving in me, when there's nothing
between us, the only sounds the stifled moans
everything is shimmery gold

There's nothing quite like how you make me
feel, entwined together to catch our breath
I feel like my soul's complete

Beating the heatwave

In summer's haze we kick off the sheets, our nakedness
a necessity because it's the fourth day over forty degrees
I watch an idea spark in your eyes – you leave our room
returning with the largest glass we own, full of ice-cubes

Our shrieks and giggles as we experiment – tracing the ice
over our skin, patterns and swirls without meaning beyond
the reaction they get – and you're so busy laughing that you
miss the moment I take a cube to begin melting on my tongue

Your laughter becomes bitten off surprise when I kiss you
the remnant of the ice slipping out of my mouth, catching
the light as it drips down your thigh, god you're gorgeous
this was a great idea I tell you , and thank you as best I can

The Luckiest

There's something sacred in how we fit together
how your hand holds mine, how your lips curve
into a smile when I've done something amusing
and the way your eyes shine bright when we dance

I could spend forever touching you
letting my hands bring you pleasure
I would spend forever loving you
pushing us higher – as long as you want

There's something magical about how we move together
about your unstifled laughter and star dimming smile
the beauty of your soul and the constant grace of your
presence, how lucky I am to have found you

My Lady

Your choice - always, but when you kneel
Before me and call me "Milady" I will not
Deny the thrill it sends through me

That you wish to submit
To serve, that you trust me
This much to give you
Orders that see us
Both sated before
The end of the night
It warms me, body and soul

Gaze into the mirror
See how I can undo
You with merely a
Touch, with a bare
Whisper - your hands
Are flexing with the
Need to touch but
You're so good for me
Keeping them to yourself

When we pull the sheets up and over
Let me take care of you in turn, now
Because it is also my joy to do so

It's a distinct...

You're so beautiful, beyond all words
with your hair unbound and your body
bare before me, the flush of heat in
your cheeks, the smile on your lips
I love how you allow me the honour
of taking you apart, how you trust
me to do right by you, the way your
lips look when I've spent ten minutes
kissing you deeply, the sounds you make
when I suck a bruise into that one spot
on your neck, how you arch into my touch
I want to worship you, tease you, lift you
up until you call my name, let me love you,
show you the depth of my endless devotion
with the tenderness of my hands, I want you
beneath me; for a moment we can pretend
I'll protect you from the world, that
you can rest easy because I'll catch you
when you fly to pieces in my arms
the only thing you need to focus
on is how good you feel, on the way
we're moving together - c'mon, let go
I want you to come for me, I want you
breathing my name like it's a prayer and
I'll do the same because the way I feel
when I'm loving you, when I'm inside of you,
it's got to be a holy thing, the way we love

**...*distinct possibility*

It is holy, this way we love - the way
I can feel how you relax when I trace
circles up and down your back, how you
stretch up to meet my lips, and laugh
when I dip you in a kiss because we are
meant for this, you are my hope, my light
and I love how much you want me, I want
you similarly even to inconvenient timing
There is something incredible about how
your body fits with mine - my hands against
your skin, how your scars feel against my
fingers, I wish that you had not endured
but I am so proud of you for doing so; for
your integrity and honour and the warmth
of your smile when I tell you these things
I want you above me, losing control while
I taste you and worship you until you give in
Let go, dear heart I've got you - I want all
you have to give, the fire and the storm
you don't have to keep it in, I have you
I love you, the sight and taste of you and
when you whisper my name, murmuring
please over and over again it makes me want
to stop teasing, to take what you're offering
give us both the high we're craving because
you are mine and I am yours and this is love

Patience

I bury my discontent deep, nothing of it shows as I set about
making you feel like you're flying, I want to see you soar

(inside I seethe, how dare someone make you ashamed
of what should have been celebrated and enjoyed)

I plan careful strategies to find the keys that let you cede
your control fully, to allow yourself to let go entirely

I am a patient person, and your pleasure is my desire
nothing about the way you enjoy yourself is shameful

and I will prove it to you, if you will let me – what matters
most in this moment is you, what you want, what you need

Guide

Your hands rest in my hair, tugging gently
guiding me to where you'd like my attention
grounding me in the moment, not-quite-pain
to cling to when I'm drowning in sensation

Undone

It's a simple act of caring

that brings us together

and yet it takes away

my breath to be

this near to you

to have this

intimacy

as your

long

hair

falls

loose

plait

un

done

surrounded

Crackling fire
warm mulled wine
a thick push rug

Lost in warmth
behind and before
surrounded by love

You complete
something in me
with jagged edges

Surrounded by love
when I whisper
your names

We are one

Let this become our peace
this passion stoked between us
this love we embrace wholeheartedly
this tenderness that brands our souls

Let this become our pleasure
our hands finding each other
our hearts beating faster
our lips meeting in love

safety

hold me down, your warm body

pressing

against mine, your hand

tightly

around my wrist and this sensation

pinned

is so enthralling, as you tease I am

safely

beneath you and able, for now, to

let

go

until the stars grow (c)old

I will remember the way you tasted
as you kissed me on the lookout
I will remember the way you smelled
like spice and warmth and *home*
I will remember the way you looked
suit jacket and bowtie without a shirt
I will remember the way you played
like everything was emotion and sound
I will remember the way that you felt
tangled in bed with nothing between us
I will remember the way that you smiled
at me like I made your dreams come true

Laughing at ourselves

We dance
badly

In the privacy of our kitchen
there's no judging eyes

So we hum waltzes while
stepping through foxtrots

Laughing
caught in the moment

Spin me into a kiss and let's take this dancing elsewhere

backrub?

tenderly tracing twisting patterns

teasing taut tendons – pressure

you moan

pressing palms seeking

pain points solving

relax

Memories made to treasure

We are private in our love – though we may tease
in public, dance a little closer than we should, give gentle
kisses and swing our hands clasped together while we walk
for us and us alone is the pleasure of undoing the other
To know the soft sounds you make when I untuck your shirt
and run my hands over your skin is my secret and mine alone
To know that you and you only will see me like this, with
nothing between me and your gaze except my hair drifting forward
and the necklace you bought me is such a thrill for my soul

I love you and we are past needing words lost in the moment
where we take our time learning anew the beauty of each other
enjoying that we have the freedom to be ourselves, that we
can have this, and nothing the world will throw at us can shake
what we share apart – my soul's thread is ever entwined with
yours and should we part you will always remain, as will the
memories of how you looked in our bed, how your gaze burned
me and for now, for now that is a distant fear and forgotten easily
when you press your lips to mine, demanding my attention again

This is forever

Stretch this moment forever with me
Warm embrace, strong arms - just be
Together, just be here, just be mine
We'll make forever from this moment in time

I will write the truths of us on my heart
My skin will carry the weight of my vow
Never to forget the ones whom I love more
Than my own self, more than my own life

So we'll make forever from small moments in time
When our lips touch, when your hand finds mine
Dream of me, dream with me – we'll be together
And stretch out this moment 'til it touches forever

Trust

Between you I rest easy
the young night, and wine,
makes the decision simple
it's the work of a moment

To shift myself and taste
salty-sweet, I love the way
you feel, love doing this,
love feeling you lose control

It's the work of a moment
one I should have expected
and this feeling of fullness
eases something lonely in my soul

you in me, me around you
trusting that you'll catch me
losing myself to the rhythm
we set gracefully between us

Taking the initiative to seek
pleasure, I strive to outlast
you both before giving in
the work of many moments

Sorrow eased

Kiss away my tears – your gentleness cradles my soul
Hold me through the long night while I grieve, while I mourn

Kiss me in the morning when the daylight has returned
that I may trust in your love and find a reason to smile again

impatiently

a full day of teasing
of watching your lips
red and curved
of watching your ass
as you dance
under glittering lights
when I finally get
my hands on you
let's not bother about
the clothes, it's easy
enough (I'm desperate)
to find skin beneath
the layers, easy enough
to kiss the smile off your lips
and take our pleasure fast

May I have this dance

There's something about the way you smile
that lights a fire in my soul - makes me *want*

Let's dance and find ourselves slipping into
that perfect alignment where we both know
just how to move together, where we're one

This is trust and beauty and fragile peace
a moment stretching beyond the reality

Let's dance together, a little closer than
we should, with arms around each other
spinning in a perfect illusion of control

asking for it

so how about this, I'll whisper all that I want to do to you
and you can tell me what you think, let me know yes or no
(not tonight is also fine – I'll ask again another time)

    so how about this, I want to hear you calling yes – I need
    it like air, your consent given, whispered and shouted and
    renewed time and time again when I ask you for it

        (you say no. you say sorry. I'll stop and tell you straight
        there's nothing to apologise for, I'd rather your honesty than
        to continue with something you do not want)

The metaphor: overused

The flower blooming, opening its soft petals
Blush pink and beautiful, dappled with dew

precious and delicate
gazed on with wonder
touched with reverence

Peace is a Lie

Lift me up and carry me to our room, lay me down on our bed
Hold me pressed against you until I'm recovered from my dread
Let me kiss you softly, take time to explore like when we were young
And new to each other; trace patterns with your hands and tongue
Stoke the flames between us high, in this moment there's only passion
Lost in the intensity of your eyes as we teach ourselves Eros' lessons

Picnic in the Rain

Our blanket sits on the grass – the hamper full of treats
Clouds mar the sky, the overcast weather grants unusual privacy
as others stay home we laugh and eat as the heavens open
Rain mists our skin, then pours down, shrugging, I pass the wine

We drink in warmth and move closer, emboldened by the
storm – we could be the last people left on earth so alone
we are and when I shiver you move and cover me with your
body, kissing me with wine-sweet breath as the rain soaks us both

When the skies clear we head home, holding hands as we
chase after the rainbow that's landed just a few feet away

fermata e caesura

everything holding
paused in balance
swell and recession

poised in perfect silence
waiting
for
the

f
  a
    l
      l

catch me

                        (always)

the dishes can wait

We pick strawberries by hand, slice them fine over ice-cream
and chocolate sauce – I cook handmade waffles to go with and
together we laugh about the healthiness of our lunch, and I'll
kiss chocolate off your lips and you'll feed me bites of waffle
In all of this perfect moment there's an overwhelming content
it steals over our limbs and we retire for an afternoon rest -
(those plans change when we're lying close in bed)

into darkness

smoky club, bass thrumming through our souls
lift me up and press me back against the wall
kiss me, uncaring of the potential of who sees
the soft press of your suit against my skin is
bliss, your strength enough to hold my weight
when you smile down at me, eyes bright with
humour and love I reach up to pull you in for
another kiss – lost in the haze there's nothing
but the way you love me and the drums beating

perfect imperfection

I didn't know it could be like this
nervous and awkward and lovely
love isn't ever perfect, loving you
isn't ever perfect but I enjoy practicing
ever so much, and by your grin when
I mention it you enjoy it as well, we
don't have anywhere to be so pull me
close and let's see if we can reach heaven

The Talk

So…

Let's talk,

take my hand

I'll look away

if it makes it easier

What is it that you want?

Because for you I'd do

pretty much anything

…

Yes, even that – with the proper words and safeties

there's no reason we can't try these things out

and darling?

Thanks for being brave enough to ask

I love you so very much

All of you

I love the way the afternoon light
gilds your skin, the way your breasts
fit in my hands, the curve of your lips
and the warmth of your embrace

Sometimes I see you standing by the desk
and I want to bend you over it, love you
intensely with all that I am, let my hands
embrace you and pull you close to me

The best thing in the world to happen to me

Sometimes (often) I wonder how you don't realise
just how attractive, how beautiful, how stunning you are
when you choose to forgo a top and bra I lose every
semblance of coherent thought because you're so gorgeous

I want to spend the rest of my days with you
to appreciate your beauty in the mornings and the night
to love your quick mind and generous spirit
to be with you as a steadfast support, someone you can lean on

I will devote myself to loving you to showing you that
everything you are is worthy of love, every time you
come over and sit by me so that I can hold your hand
and talk about everything and nothing until it's midnight
makes me more and more sure that there's no-one I love more

Fire in the Soul

This slow burning fire roars up high – and there's a chance we'll die tomorrow so tonight let's make love and forget about everything else touch me gently, make my body sing – let me tangle my hands in your hair, let me press kisses across your skin, let me touch, make me tremble – nothing between us as we press skin to skin and kiss until we're breathless, laughing and sighing – the sounds we make are a holy hymn of appreciation, because this right here is divinity ablaze

In every season

When summer comes with its heavy heat and a birthday you
would rather us forget I will be there with ice-cream to share
and shower you with affection for no reason at all

When autumn brings its storms I'll go dancing in the rain with you
and kiss your smiling lips, rejoicing in the way your mood lifts as
the leaves drift down and the wind whispers secret joys

When winter nights grow cold I'll hold you close under the blankets
Let you rest your cold feet on my thighs to warm them because I love
you, with your freezing extremities and all

And when spring comes with all its flowers and its newness blooming
I will pick petals from roses, lay you down upon them and love you
until we both forget our names in the brilliance of our joy.

Let me…

Let me undress you – slide off the jacket and undo the tie
seek the softness of your skin, chasing the buttons down

Let me undress you, undo the buttons you can't reach
help you step out of the froth of skirts as they pool beneath us

Let me love you with tender hands tracing the curves seeking
out the secret curves and planes you hid away beneath the layers

Let me love you with passionate hands to touch and stroke
finding all the ways to make blushes bloom on your skin

The many desires you stir to life

I want to bend you over our bed
take you hard and fast while you bite
back your screams and sighs

I want to push you up against
the kitchen counter and scandalise
the neighbours if they dare to look

I want to love you slow and careful
in the morning when we've both
just woken up to face the day

I want to push higher, give you
everything and more each night
and then fall asleep entangled

We know ourselves complete

Nothing about how we love is impersonal
I would know you without my eyes
by the tenderness of your touch,
the gentleness of your movement,
by every breath you fight to keep even
control tested by tightening coils of desire

we lock eyes, a thousand words unsaid between us

Then you grin at me, move faster than you should be able to
Pressing me into the soft mattress, kissing me as your hands roam
I make no objection, choose to guide towards my specific desires
You are rarely led but for now, you follow – I sigh, pleased as all
thought is lost to the talent residing in your clever fingers

Storm warning

We are a storm raging
the flashes of lightning
the rolling thunder
the striking rain

We are – in this moment subsumed
so close to becoming one, we are
movement and sound and emotion

We enter the eye
the golden light
time stretching
waiting for the fall

And love is...

To be adored and shared and celebrated
to find in ones alike and different our
shared humanity which isn't sex, nor romance
but love – that which flies beyond the infinite
that which burns bright as the stars at night
that which comes to life between people
of any gender, any race, any religion
because love isn't just sex, love is family
and friends that become more like family
and love is finding someone you want to
spend time with because you love to be
with them and love is love is love – it makes
us stronger and weaker, brings us together
gives us hope that we are not alone, makes
us want to be better, to change the world

and we can

A Favoured Number

> I appreciate your beauty when you're
> In between my thighs, the look in your
> Eyes as you tease, but I want tonight
> To be for the both of us, you rise up
> And kiss me, asking without words
> So I'll whisper the question in your ear
> Watch your smile bloom as you shift
> Allowing me to give you the same gift
> To lick and tease, to find a rhythm that
> Allows us to change to a duet, our hands
> playing our bodies like instruments
> Nothing can break the moment we have
> Seized for ourselves as we make love